This book belongs to:

____

Phone: ____________________

Description of Piece:

Date Started: ***Finished:***

Clay Used:

Technique Used:

Firings: bisque/ earthenware/ stoneware

underglaze/ oxides/ glazes used:

Design

Notes:

Things to remember next time:

Description of Piece: ______________________

____

____

Date Started: ______________ ***Finished:*** ______________

Clay Used: ______________________

Technique Used: ______________________

Firings: bisque/ earthenware/ stoneware

____

____

underglaze/ oxides/ glazes used: ______________________

____

____

Design

Notes:

Things to remember next time:

Description of Piece:

Date Started: ***Finished:***

Clay Used:

Technique Used:

Firings: bisque/ earthenware/ stoneware

underglaze/ oxides/ glazes used:

Design

Notes:

Things to remember next time:

Description of Piece: ______________________

____

____

Date Started: ____________ ***Finished:*** ____________

____

Clay Used: ______________________

____

Technique Used: ______________________

____

Firings: bisque/ earthenware/ stoneware

____

____

underglaze/ oxides/ glazes used: ______________________

____

____

Design

Notes:

Things to remember next time:

Description of Piece:

Date Started: ***Finished:***

Clay Used:

Technique Used:

Firings: bisque/ earthenware/ stoneware

underglaze/ oxides/ glazes used:

Design

Notes:

Things to remember next time:

Description of Piece: ______________________________

____

____

Date Started: ______________ ***Finished:*** ______________

____

Clay Used: ______________________________

____

Technique Used: ______________________________

____

Firings: bisque/ earthenware/ stoneware

____

____

underglaze/ oxides/ glazes used: ______________________

____

____

Design

Notes:

Things to remember next time:

Description of Piece:

Date Started: ***Finished:***

Clay Used:

Technique Used:

Firings: bisque/ earthenware/ stoneware

underglaze/ oxides/ glazes used:

Design

Notes:

Things to remember next time:

Description of Piece:

Date Started: ***Finished:***

Clay Used:

Technique Used:

Firings: bisque/ earthenware/ stoneware

underglaze/ oxides/ glazes used:

Design

Notes:

Things to remember next time:

Description of Piece: ______________________

Date Started: ______________ *Finished:* ______________

Clay Used: ______________________

Technique Used: ______________________

Firings: bisque/ earthenware/ stoneware

underglaze/ oxides/ glazes used: ______________

Design

Notes:

Things to remember next time:

Description of Piece:

Date Started: ***Finished:***

Clay Used:

Technique Used:

Firings: bisque/ earthenware/ stoneware

underglaze/ oxides/ glazes used:

Design

Notes:

Things to remember next time:

Description of Piece:

Date Started: ***Finished:***

Clay Used:

Technique Used:

Firings: bisque/ earthenware/ stoneware

underglaze/ oxides/ glazes used:

Design

Notes:

Things to remember next time:

Description of Piece:

Date Started: ***Finished:***

Clay Used:

Technique Used:

Firings: bisque/ earthenware/ stoneware

underglaze/ oxides/ glazes used:

Design

Notes:

Things to remember next time:

Description of Piece: ______

Date Started: ______ ***Finished:*** ______

Clay Used: ______

Technique Used: ______

Firings: bisque/ earthenware/ stoneware

underglaze/ oxides/ glazes used: ______

Design

Notes:

Things to remember next time:

Description of Piece: ______________________

____

____

Date Started: ____________ ***Finished:*** ____________

____

Clay Used: ______________________

____

Technique Used: ______________________

____

Firings: bisque/ earthenware/ stoneware

____

____

underglaze/ oxides/ glazes used: ______________________

____

____

Design

Notes:

Things to remember next time:

Description of Piece: ___

Date Started: ___ ***Finished:*** ___

Clay Used: ___

Technique Used: ___

Firings: bisque/ earthenware/ stoneware

underglaze/ oxides/ glazes used: ___

Design

Notes:

Things to remember next time:

Description of Piece:

Date Started: ***Finished:***

Clay Used:

Technique Used:

Firings: bisque/ earthenware/ stoneware

underglaze/ oxides/ glazes used:

Design

Notes:

Things to remember next time:

Description of Piece: ______________________________

Date Started: ______________ ***Finished:*** ______________

Clay Used: ______________________________

Technique Used: ______________________________

Firings: bisque/ earthenware/ stoneware

underglaze/ oxides/ glazes used: ______________________________

Design

Notes:

Things to remember next time:

Description of Piece: ______________________

Date Started: ____________ ***Finished:*** ____________

Clay Used: ______________________

Technique Used: ______________________

Firings: bisque/ earthenware/ stoneware

underglaze/ oxides/ glazes used: ______________________

Design

Notes:

Things to remember next time:

Description of Piece:

Date Started: *Finished:*

Clay Used:

Technique Used:

Firings: bisque/ earthenware/ stoneware

underglaze/ oxides/ glazes used:

Design

Notes:

Things to remember next time:

Description of Piece: ______________________________

____

Date Started: ______________ ***Finished:*** ______________

Clay Used: ______________________________

Technique Used: ______________________________

Firings: bisque/ earthenware/ stoneware

____

underglaze/ oxides/ glazes used: ______________________________

____

Design

Notes:

Things to remember next time:

Description of Piece: ______________________

____

____

Date Started: ______________ ***Finished:*** ______________

____

Clay Used: ______________________

____

Technique Used: ______________________

____

Firings: bisque/ earthenware/ stoneware

____

____

underglaze/ oxides/ glazes used: ______________________

____

____

Design

Notes:

Things to remember next time:

Description of Piece: ______________________

____

____

Date Started: ______________ ***Finished:*** ______________

____

Clay Used: ______________________

____

Technique Used: ______________________

____

Firings: bisque/ earthenware/ stoneware

____

____

underglaze/ oxides/ glazes used: ______________________

____

____

Design

Notes:

Things to remember next time:

Description of Piece: ______

Date Started: ______ ***Finished:*** ______

Clay Used: ______

Technique Used: ______

Firings: bisque/ earthenware/ stoneware

underglaze/ oxides/ glazes used: ______

Design

Notes:

Things to remember next time:

Description of Piece: ______________________

____

____

Date Started: ____________ *Finished:* ____________

____

Clay Used: ______________________

____

Technique Used: ______________________

____

Firings: bisque/ earthenware/ stoneware

____

____

underglaze/ oxides/ glazes used: ______________________

____

____

Design

Notes:

Things to remember next time:

Description of Piece:

Date Started: ***Finished:***

Clay Used:

Technique Used:

Firings: bisque/ earthenware/ stoneware

underglaze/ oxides/ glazes used:

Design

Notes:

Things to remember next time:

Description of Piece: ______

Date Started: ______ ***Finished:*** ______

Clay Used: ______

Technique Used: ______

Firings: bisque/ earthenware/ stoneware

underglaze/ oxides/ glazes used: ______

Design

Notes:

Things to remember next time:

Description of Piece:

Date Started: ***Finished:***

Clay Used:

Technique Used:

Firings: bisque/ earthenware/ stoneware

underglaze/ oxides/ glazes used:

Design

Notes:

Things to remember next time:

Description of Piece: ______________________

____

____

Date Started: ______________ ***Finished:*** ______________

____

Clay Used: ______________________

____

Technique Used: ______________________

____

Firings: bisque/ earthenware/ stoneware

____

____

underglaze/ oxides/ glazes used: ______________________

____

____

Design

Notes:

Things to remember next time:

Description of Piece:

Date Started: ***Finished:***

Clay Used:

Technique Used:

Firings: bisque/ earthenware/ stoneware

underglaze/ oxides/ glazes used:

Design

Notes:

Things to remember next time:

Description of Piece: ______

______

Date Started: ______ ***Finished:*** ______

Clay Used: ______

Technique Used: ______

Firings: bisque/ earthenware/ stoneware

______

underglaze/ oxides/ glazes used: ______

______

Design

Notes:

Things to remember next time:

Description of Piece:

Date Started: *Finished:*

Clay Used:

Technique Used:

Firings: bisque/ earthenware/ stoneware

underglaze/ oxides/ glazes used:

Design

Notes:

Things to remember next time:

Description of Piece: ____________________

____

____

Date Started: ____________ ***Finished:*** ____________

____

Clay Used: ____________________

____

Technique Used: ____________________

____

Firings: bisque/ earthenware/ stoneware

____

____

underglaze/ oxides/ glazes used: ____________________

____

____

Design

Notes:

Things to remember next time:

Description of Piece:

Date Started: ***Finished:***

Clay Used:

Technique Used:

Firings: bisque/ earthenware/ stoneware

underglaze/ oxides/ glazes used:

Design

Notes:

Things to remember next time:

Description of Piece:

Date Started: ***Finished:***

Clay Used:

Technique Used:

Firings: bisque/ earthenware/ stoneware

underglaze/ oxides/ glazes used:

Design

Notes:

Things to remember next time:

Description of Piece: ______________________

____

____

Date Started: ______________ ***Finished:*** ______________

____

Clay Used: ______________________

____

Technique Used: ______________________

____

Firings: bisque/ earthenware/ stoneware

____

____

underglaze/ oxides/ glazes used: ______________________

____

____

Design

Notes:

Things to remember next time:

Description of Piece:

Date Started: ***Finished:***

Clay Used:

Technique Used:

Firings: bisque/ earthenware/ stoneware

underglaze/ oxides/ glazes used:

Design

Notes:

Things to remember next time:

Description of Piece: ______________________

____

____

Date Started: ____________ ***Finished:*** ____________

____

Clay Used: ______________________

____

Technique Used: ______________________

____

Firings: bisque/ earthenware/ stoneware

____

____

underglaze/ oxides/ glazes used: ______________________

____

____

Design

Notes:

Things to remember next time:

Description of Piece: ____________________

Date Started: __________ ***Finished:*** __________

Clay Used: ____________________

Technique Used: ____________________

Firings: bisque/ earthenware/ stoneware

underglaze/ oxides/ glazes used: ____________________

Design

Notes:

Things to remember next time:

Description of Piece:

Date Started: ***Finished:***

Clay Used:

Technique Used:

Firings: bisque/ earthenware/ stoneware

underglaze/ oxides/ glazes used:

Design

Notes:

Things to remember next time:

Description of Piece: ______________________________

____

____

Date Started: ______________ ***Finished:*** __________

____

Clay Used: _________________________________

____

Technique Used: _____________________________

____

Firings: bisque/ earthenware/ stoneware

____

____

underglaze/ oxides/ glazes used: _______________

____

____

Design

Notes:

Things to remember next time:

Description of Piece: ____________________

Date Started: __________ ***Finished:*** __________

Clay Used: ____________________

Technique Used: ____________________

Firings: bisque/ earthenware/ stoneware

underglaze/ oxides/ glazes used: __________

Design

Notes:

Things to remember next time:

Description of Piece: ______________________

____

Date Started: ______________ ***Finished:*** __________

Clay Used: ______________________

Technique Used: ______________________

Firings: bisque/ earthenware/ stoneware

____

underglaze/ oxides/ glazes used: ______________

____

Design

Notes:

Things to remember next time:

Description of Piece: ______________________

____

____

Date Started: ______________ ***Finished:*** __________

____

Clay Used: ______________________

____

Technique Used: ______________________

____

Firings: bisque/ earthenware/ stoneware

____

____

underglaze/ oxides/ glazes used: ______________

____

____

Design

Notes:

Things to remember next time:

Description of Piece: ______________________

____

____

Date Started: ____________ ***Finished:*** ____________

____

Clay Used: ______________________

____

Technique Used: ______________________

____

Firings: bisque/ earthenware/ stoneware

____

____

underglaze/ oxides/ glazes used: ______________________

____

____

Design

Notes:

Things to remember next time:

Description of Piece: ____________________

____

____

Date Started: ______________ ***Finished:*** ____________

____

Clay Used: ________________________________

____

Technique Used: ___________________________

____

Firings: bisque/ earthenware/ stoneware

____

____

underglaze/ oxides/ glazes used: _____________

____

____

Design

Notes:

Things to remember next time:

Description of Piece:

Date Started: ***Finished:***

Clay Used:

Technique Used:

Firings: bisque/ earthenware/ stoneware

underglaze/ oxides/ glazes used:

Design

Notes:

Things to remember next time:

Description of Piece: ______________________

____

____

Date Started: ______________ ***Finished:*** ______________

____

Clay Used: ______________________

____

Technique Used: ______________________

____

Firings: bisque/ earthenware/ stoneware

____

____

underglaze/ oxides/ glazes used: ______________________

____

____

Design

Notes:

Things to remember next time:

Description of Piece: ______________________

____

____

Date Started: ____________ ***Finished:*** ____________

____

Clay Used: ______________________

____

Technique Used: ______________________

____

Firings: bisque/ earthenware/ stoneware

____

____

underglaze/ oxides/ glazes used: ______________________

____

____

Design

Notes:

Things to remember next time:

Description of Piece: ___________

Date Started: ___________ ***Finished:*** ___________

Clay Used: ___________

Technique Used: ___________

Firings: bisque/ earthenware/ stoneware

underglaze/ oxides/ glazes used: ___________

Design

Notes:

Things to remember next time:

Description of Piece: ______________________________

____

____

Date Started: ______________ ***Finished:*** ______________

____

Clay Used: ______________________________

____

Technique Used: ______________________________

____

Firings: bisque/ earthenware/ stoneware

____

____

underglaze/ oxides/ glazes used: ______________

____

____

Design

Notes:

Things to remember next time:

Description of Piece: ______________________

____

Date Started: __________ ***Finished:*** __________

Clay Used: ______________________

Technique Used: ______________________

Firings: bisque/ earthenware/ stoneware

____

underglaze/ oxides/ glazes used: ______________________

____

Design

Notes:

Things to remember next time:

Pottery Essentials

Made in United States
Orlando, FL
04 November 2024